jump
at de sun

jump at de sun

 the story of
Zora Neale Hurston

by A. P. PORTER

foreword by

LUCY ANN HURSTON

 Carolrhoda Books, Inc./Minneapolis

To Janice

I am grateful to Lucy Ann Hurston for her invaluable corrections and irreplaceable photographs. Many thanks to Marybeth Lorbiecki, my editor; Zachary Marell, the designer for this project; and Lynn Olsen, photo researcher extraordinaire. And thanks to Alice Walker for waking all of us up.

A.P.P.

The cover photograph was taken on Zora's graduation from Morgan Academy (high school) at the age of twenty-seven. The painting is of Eatonville, done by Jules Andre Smith.

First Avenue Editions, an imprint of Lerner Publishing Group
241 First Avenue North
Minneapolis, MN 55401 U.S.A.

Website address: www.lernerbooks.com

Library of Congress Cataloging-in-Publication Data

Porter, A. P.
  Jump at de sun : the story of Zora Neale Hurston / by A. P. Porter; with a foreword by Lucy Ann Hurston.
      p. cm.
  Includes bibliographical references and index.
  Summary: Follows the life of the Afro-American writer known for her novels, plays, articles, and collections of folklore.
  ISBN 0-87614-546-2 (pbk. : alk. paper)
  1. Hurston, Zora Neale—Biography—Juvenile literature. 2. Novelists, American—20th century—Biography—Juvenile literature. 3. Folklorists—United States—Biography—Juvenile literature. 4. Afro-Americans—Intellectual life—Juvenile literature. [1. Hurston, Zora Neale. 2. Authors, American. 3. Afro-Americans—Biography.] I. Title. II. Title: Jump at de sun.
PS3515.U789Z83 1992
813'.52—dc20   91-37241

Manufactured in the United States of America
4 5 6 7 8 9 – JR – 07 06 05 04 03 02

ᐯᐧᐯᐧ *contents* ᐅᐧᐅᐧ

foreword

Aunt Zora died when I was a toddler, but I remember stories about her. And I remember the way my father's eyes would light up when he talked about her.

When I was nine years old, I found her in my attic, neatly tucked away in the dusty part I was not allowed to enter. I would click the light switch over and over until it worked. I would climb the creaky stairs. The attic smelled safe, different from the rest of our house. It reminded me of her. Like coming in by the fire after playing too long in the snow. Like coming home.

I would wipe a place in the dust to sit, and I would talk to her. I told her things no one else knew. And she spoke to me through her books—*Dust Tracks on a Road, Mules and Men, Their Eyes Were Watching God.* I didn't understand the titles, but it didn't matter. She seemed to have written about us—my family and our friends. We didn't talk like the people in her books, but we thought many of the same things. She knew me. Sometimes I had to cover my mouth so my family wouldn't hear me up there laughing. Sometimes I would cry. Aunt Zora was a feast.

Zora was known for her generosity, funny stories, and outrageous actions, as well as her hot temper and strong opinions. Zora had such a powerful personality that one friend said, "Zora would have been Zora even if she'd been an Eskimo."

The road for an African American has always been uphill. Aunt Zora didn't care. In some ways, a woman has always had a tougher time than a man. She didn't care about that either. Aunt Zora just would not quit. Her courage and persistence inspired me to go back to school, to write, to lecture, to jump at the sun.

Lucy Ann Hurston
daughter of Everette Hurston,
Zora's youngest brother

🎵🎵 *author's note* 🎵🎵

In the early 1900s, most people in the United States saw African culture as something to be overcome. Black people were said to be only capable of working for white people. For hundreds of years, white people had simply left Africans out of history books. Black and white people had come to think that Africans had never achieved anything.

Many people didn't know that African societies and traditions even existed. European society was thought to be the best in the world, and surely everyone wanted to be like the best. So people who did things differently were *backward*. Many African Americans were ashamed of their color and their African heritage.

On January 7, 1891, Zora Neale Hurston was born into a nation where African Americans were feared and hated. Between Hurston's birth and her tenth birthday, white people in the United States publicly murdered—lynched—1,116 African Americans. They killed 69 in Florida alone. Black people were killed for all sorts of reasons, from being successful in business to talking back to a white person. Many victims were tortured; some were burned alive.

But Hurston grew up in Eatonville, Florida, a warm black island of respect and love. She learned to be sure of herself and proud of her personal worth. Hurston knew that African Americans were *different,* not inferior.

Once outside of Eatonville, Hurston encountered white racism. And she was poor all her life; the most money she earned from a book was $943.75. But when she died, Zora Neale Hurston had written four published novels, two books of folklore, and an autobiography; as well as many magazine articles, essays, short stories, and plays. In an essay, "How It Feels to be Colored Me," Hurston wrote, "Sometimes I feel discriminated against, but it does not make me angry. It merely astonishes me. How can any [people] deny themselves the pleasure of my company?" I can't imagine.

In the African-American town of Eatonville, Florida, everybody had
lush gardens and yards. People visited a great deal, so they knew their
neighbors' names and their business. This scene from the early 1900s
was captured by painter Jules Andre Smith.

the garden gate

In the dappled shade of the chinaberry trees, Zora Hurston jumped up on the garden gate. Her sister and two of her brothers lay in the sunny yard, near a mound of eggshells on the grass.

Whop! A rubbery boiled egg bounced off Zora's head and wobbled off in the dust. Thup! Another caught her on the back of her grass-stained dress.

Zora leapt down from her perch and raced around the Cape Jasmine bushes that lined the front walk. She went straight for the rest of the eggs, scooped one up, and let it fly.

Sarah got it on her ear and howled. Zora smiled her satisfaction. Dick had probably been the one who hit her. But prim Miss Sarah needed an egg on her ear.

Grinning, Zora climbed back up on the gate to keep an eye on the road and try to hitch a ride. She didn't want to miss anybody. White folks were always going to and from Orlando, and they were usually willing to give her a lift. She wouldn't go far, just down the road a piece. For Zora, the garden gate was a stage, a good place to wave from. She might get a spanking, but it would be worth it.

Inside the gate was Zora's world—her sister and six brothers; and her parents, John and Lucy. The big garden kept the family well fed. Oranges, tangerines, and grapefruits grew right there in the yard. And their house was as roomy as their huge yard. After all, it was Reverend Hurston's house.

John Hurston had moved in near the beginning of Eatonville, the United States' first official African-American town. He had even written some of the town's laws. John had come a long way.

Back in Notasulga, Alabama, Reverend John Cornelius Hurston II had come from "over the creek." Lucy's mother, Sarah, had never liked him. Yes, he'd learned to read, and yes, he was a Baptist minister. But he was still just a nineteen-year-old sharecropper working for poor white trash. People said his father was a certain local white man. John's light brown skin and gray-green eyes said so too. To Mrs. Potts, John would always be "dat yaller bastard."

One Sunday in 1881, at the Macedonia Baptist Church, John Hurston had spied Sarah Potts's daughter. Lucy Potts was fifteen years old and the freshest girl in Notasulga. John couldn't help seeing chocolate-brown Lucy up there in the choir loft. He could hardly see anything else. He took to hanging around her like a puppy—a muscular, two-hundred-pound puppy. John had it bad. He sent Lucy notes stuck between the pages of hymnbooks. Lucy decided to marry him just so she could get some peace. The Potts family said no, but Lucy said yes anyway. Lucy's mother wouldn't come to the wedding or even let Lucy come back home to visit.

After the wedding, John and Lucy Hurston moved into their own cabin on a nearby plantation. John worked for the white man who owned the place, and Lucy had babies—Hezekiah Robert and John III in the first three years. Then along came Richard and Sarah. It got to be harder and harder just to feed everybody. And for John, working on a white man's plantation offered no future worth thinking about.

When Zora was born on January 7, 1891, John was out of town. The midwife was at a hog killing, so when the time came, Lucy sent one of the children to fetch her. But Zora didn't wait. Lucy gave birth to Zora all alone. Afterward, Lucy was too weak even to pick up her new baby. Luckily, a white friend of the family happened by. He cut the cord, cleaned Zora up, tied a belly band on her to help her navel heal, and handed her over to Lucy.

When John returned and learned that Zora had had the nerve to be born a girl, he threatened to cut his own throat. He didn't, but he never let Zora forget his disappointment either. Sarah was all the girls he needed.

John and Lucy had five children now. John *had* to find a better way to make a living. So he left Alabama.

Some of the hardworking folk from Eatonville had jobs at nearby plantations.

Zora's parents, Lucy (Lula) Potts Hurston and the Reverend John Hurston, Eatonville's preacher. Their marriage was a stormy one, though Zora concluded that they "were really in love."

He didn't know exactly what he was looking for, but he'd know it when he found it. After making his way to Florida, he heard about a purely colored town that was trying to get itself founded. An African-American town sounded like a fine idea. When John found it, he decided to stay there—in Eatonville, Florida.

After a year or so of doing carpentry for other newcomers to Eatonville, John had earned enough money to send for his family. Lucy brought only the children and her bed. That was enough. The Hurstons were together again.

Five miles from Orlando, Eatonville was "a city of five lakes, three croquet courts, three hundred brown skins, three hundred good swimmers, plenty guavas, two schools, and no jail house." No white people lived there.

The Eatonville of Zora's childhood was a warm, accepting place for African Americans to grow up in. Children from all over the neighborhood played at the Hurston place. Lucy didn't like her children to play anywhere else. She thought it would look like they didn't have enough home to make staying there worthwhile.

Reverend John Hurston was soon *Mayor* Hurston, so the Hurstons were part of Eatonville's upper crust. John was a moderator of the South Florida Baptist Association, and important church people often stayed at the house. Visitors usually came for supper; sometimes they stayed overnight. Visitors or no, there was always a passel of children.

Sarah, his elder girl, was John's favorite child, and he made no bones about it. John would seldom let Lucy spank Sarah. If Sarah needed a spanking, he said he would tend to her. She just never seemed to need one. Sarah's quiet daintiness called out for frilly dresses and showy ribbons.

Zora was John's least favorite child. John and his younger daughter just could *not* get along. Forward, outspoken, always wanting to "wear de big hat," Zora was everything John thought a girl child should *not* be. John Hurston *knew* what happened to colored people who spoke up for themselves. Zora wrote that her father believed "it did not do for Negroes to have too much spirit. He was always threatening to break mine or kill me in the attempt."

Lucy's mother agreed with John about one thing only— Zora. Sarah Potts said that Zora was the curse God had put on Lucy for marrying John. Zora was too uppity. Mother Potts had been a slave, and she couldn't get used to the idea of even looking a white person in the eye. And Zora waved them down on the road, begging for rides! Who did she think she was?

But Lucy Hurston didn't want to "squinch" Zora's spirit. Lucy told all her children to "jump at de sun!" Zora wrote, "We might not land on the sun, but at least we would get off the ground." Lucy hadn't had much schooling, but she held regular classes for her children at home. She was the teacher through long division and parsing sentences. Then Hezekiah Robert, called Bob, took over. Lucy stuck around to keep order.

Before Zora was seven years old, she began having visions, twelve scenes in a row. She could see herself and what was happening as clear as anything. Zora was sure it would all come true. She saw that she would be a homeless orphan, that her family would split up, that she would be sad and lonely. Zora felt set apart from other children. The visions gave her power that she didn't want, "knowledge before its time."

When Zora was in the fifth grade at the Hungerford School, two white women from Minnesota visited her classroom. They heard Zora read aloud, and she impressed them mightily with her skill. When the women got back to Minnesota, they sent Zora a box full of books, some by Rudyard Kipling, Robert Louis Stevenson, and the Grimm brothers. Now she could read Roman and Greek myths and Norse legends. All those books for her!

With her new books, Zora began to see Eatonville as dull and ordinary. She was a world traveler in the body of a little girl. Zora never stopped heading for the horizon, the "belly band of the world." Hitching a ride from the garden gate was only practice. Lucy said someone must have spread "travel dust" around the doorstep the day Zora was born. Zora wrote, "My soul was with the gods and my body in the village."

Zora's body and soul found common ground at Joe Clarke's store. A plain wooden building with a porch across the front, the general store was the heart of Eatonville. Everybody had to go there sooner or later for something or other. Whenever Zora got to go, she listened as hard as she could, dawdling her way past the men gathered on the front porch. She tried to disappear into the shadows, so the grown-ups wouldn't shoo her away. All the news and gossip for miles around passed by there. Zora's ears did a lot of growing up on Joe Clarke's porch.

Stories about animals that talked, slavery, creation, and the doings of the night before all paraded over the porch of Joe Clarke's store. When a guitar or mouth harp was pulled out, everyone would sing and stomp.

Zora's favorite times at Joe Clarke's were the "lying" sessions. That was when men tried to outdo each other telling folktales—stories that folks told each other over and over for years and years. The stories about Brer Rabbit and Brer Fox and Sis Cat and Brer Bear and Lion and Buzzard and Tiger and Sis Snail were some of Zora's lifelong loves.

Some lies were the truth stretched out for effect. Some lies were from scratch. But they were all just stories and not to be taken for the exact truth. Zora took the stories seriously and began to make up her own. When Zora told her mother about talking with a beautiful bird and walking on water, Lucy just listened and smiled.

Zora's imagination worked even on trees. She talked and sang with a "loving pine" that "had a mighty fine bass voice when it really took a notion to let it out." She wrote that another tree put on a skull head at dusk and crept close to the house to threaten her.

To Zora, the leafy covering of an ear of corn was "Miss Corn Shuck." Miss Corn Shuck's gentleman friend, "Mr. Sweet Smell," was a bar of soap that Lucy had been saving for company. Another woman, "Miss Corn Cob," pined for Mr. Sweet Smell, and made as much trouble between him and Miss Corn Shuck as she could. Zora eventually outgrew Miss Corn Cob and Mr. Sweet Smell, but she never outgrew the folktales she heard on the porch of Joe Clarke's store. She used those tall tales even after she grew up, changing them, adding to them, smooshing them together.

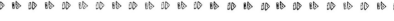

jacksonville and jim crow

In 1904, when Zora was thirteen years old, Lucy Hurston went back to Alabama. Dinky, Lucy's sister, was awfully sick, and Lucy wanted to be there to help out. Lucy had other things weighing on her mind too.

Lucy's mother had never forgiven her for marrying John. That still bothered Lucy. And some years before, Lucy's favorite nephew, Jimmie, had been murdered —his headless body dumped on the railroad tracks. Being home again reminded Lucy of her grief. All that, and watching her sister die before her eyes, just wore Lucy down. When she got back to Eatonville, she was ailing badly. The family later called her illness the "death cold."

When someone was dying in that part of the South, it was customary to remove the pillow from under the head, so as to make death easier. Clock faces in the room were to be hidden; otherwise, they'd stop working when the dying person's time ran out. Mirrors must be covered so they wouldn't take on a permanent image of the corpse. The deathbed had to face east, the direction that the world turns.

Lucy didn't want any of those things done for her — don't cover the mirror, don't turn the bed east, don't hide the clocks, and leave the pillow alone. On her deathbed, Lucy gave Zora careful instructions. Zora promised to do as her mother said.

But Zora was only a child. She was no match for the will of her father and the other adults of Eatonville. Zora was playing in the yard when she saw several women go into the house. She followed them. As Zora slipped into her mother's bedroom, the adults were turning the bed so Lucy would face east. Someone began covering the clock face. Another hand reached out to remove Lucy's pillow.

"Don't!" Zora screamed. But her father held her, and the others "frowned [her] down." Zora watched as all the death rites were done as her mother lay helpless, unable to speak. In later years, Zora wrote, "I hope that Mama knows that I did my best. She must know how I have suffered for my failure. . . . That hour began my wanderings."

Two weeks after her mother was buried, Zora had to leave home for the first time. John sent Zora to join Sarah and Bob at a boarding school in Jacksonville, Florida.

At school, Zora tried to learn everything and meet everybody at once. She made a true pest of herself, hanging around the older girls at school and generally getting in the way.

It was in Jacksonville that Zora discovered "Jim Crow." That was the name given to customs and laws that kept African Americans and European Americans apart, or segregated. Zora said that in Jacksonville the "white people had funny ways."

White people forced black people to use water fountains, toilets, and schools that were separate from those of white people. If a movie theater let colored people in at all, they had to sit high up in the balcony. On buses, African Americans had to sit in the back; European Americans sat in the front. On trains, colored people had separate cars, up near the engine where the most smoke and noise were. The ways of white folks were funny indeed.

These scenes from Florida in the early 1900s show how Jim Crow laws kept "coloreds" separate from "whites." Zora hated the discrimination of these laws, and in the 1940s, she wrote, "I am for complete repeal of all Jim Crow laws in the U.S. once and for all, and right now."

The white folks around Eatonville had welcomed Zora into their homes. So Zora was shocked to meet white people who weren't fans of hers. Zora wrote later, "Jacksonville made me know that I was a little colored girl."

After Zora had been in Jacksonville a couple of months, Sarah said she was sick and wanted to go home. Not long after Sarah left, Zora got a letter from her. Their father had married again.

That was too much. Why couldn't he have waited? Why didn't he show some respect for their mother? He shouldn't have married again so soon. It just wasn't right. And Sarah said so.

John's new wife, Mattie, was so angry about Sarah's impudence that she made John put his daughter out of the house.

And Mattie still wasn't satisfied. She insisted that John go over to where Sarah was staying and beat her with a buggy whip. For the first time, John Hurston hit Sarah. Even then, he hit her only once. But that was enough. Zora wrote, "Neither Papa nor Sarah ever looked at each other in the same way again. . . . As for me, . . . it made a tiger out of me. . . . It made me miserable to see Sarah look like that." Zora made up her mind to even the score someday.

While Sarah and her father were falling out, Zora was unhappy in Jacksonville. There was no playing ball with the boys, no woods, no lakes, and most of all, "just a jagged hole where my home used to be."

Then, just as Zora was getting used to her new life,

she learned that her room and meals had not been paid for. So the school's vice president put her to work. Zora had to pay her own way, scrubbing the stairs and helping out in the kitchen. Just the same, the vice president hassled Zora for money and embarrassed her in front of the other pupils. Zora wrote, "That used to keep me shrunk up inside. I got so I wouldn't play too hard. . . . My spirits would not have quite so far to fall."

In the spring of 1905, after the other pupils had gone home for the summer, Zora's father still hadn't sent for her. Maybe he'd forgotten her. He'd never liked her. Maybe he didn't want her to come back.

He didn't. John Hurston finally wrote to the school suggesting the officials adopt Zora. The school couldn't do that. Her mother was dead, her father didn't want her, and Zora had to go back to Eatonville anyway. She had nowhere else to go.

John Hurston's house was no longer home to Zora. Her four older siblings had left for good. And Mattie Hurston had set about getting rid of the rest. Soon the last of the Hurston children were scattered too—gone to live with Lucy's friends in Eatonville.

Zora was shunted among relatives and friends for more than five years. She was miserable. She felt unloved. She had little to read, and she went to school only sometimes. She had no home and knew no peace. "There is something about poverty that smells like death," she wrote later. "People can be slave-ships in shoes." Still, Zora was a choosy beggar and as mouthy as ever. Being needy didn't make her humble.

When she was about nineteen years old, Zora tried housework to earn a living. She'd always looked younger than she was, though, and many housewives wouldn't hire her because they thought she would be irresponsible. They were right.

Zora was easily distracted. She spent a lot of time reading her employers' books rather than cleaning their houses. But children loved her—she was a great storyteller.

Eventually, Zora got a job as a maid. The children of the family loved her so much that the job turned into full-time babysitting. But the older housekeeper resented her easy duties and demanded that Zora be fired. She was.

Zora got fired from a lot of jobs over the years. Sometimes she didn't like her employers. Sometimes they didn't like her. She got fired just the same.

Meanwhile, Zora's brother Dick had married. He wanted Zora to come live with him and his wife in Sanford, Florida, and he sent her a railroad ticket for the trip. Her spirits soared at the thought of being with her family again. She might even be able to go to school!

But Zora had no sooner gotten to Sanford when her father ordered her to come stay with him in Eatonville. John Hurston's orders still meant something, and Zora went.

the last straw

Zora found her father a changed man, less lively. His spirit seemed smaller. She wrote, "Papa's shoulders began to get tired." He had once been a respected man in the town he had helped build. John Hurston didn't walk tall anymore.

Zora's stepmother had expected to be looked up to as the wife of Reverend Hurston. Instead, Mattie Hurston's new neighbors despised her. Then Mattie got rid of her stepchildren. Folks thought even less of her after that. As for John, he had sent his own children away on Mattie's say-so. Folks thought less of him too. Most of all, John thought less of himself.

One Monday morning in about 1910, Mattie tried to make John whip Zora for her sassiness. Suddenly, John had had enough. He'd already put Sarah out for not showing enough respect for his new wife. He wasn't about to make the same mistake twice. He refused.

Zora's stepmother, Mattie Hurston, posing with John Hurston in 1907

Enraged, Mattie threw a bottle at Zora's head.

"She never should have missed," Zora wrote. "I wanted her blood and plenty of it."

Zora rushed across the room and commenced to beating Mattie's head against the wall. Mattie scratched Zora and pulled her hair, but Zora was too angry and too strong. Mattie had to settle for spitting in Zora's face. Zora punched Mattie out while John stood by, pleading with Zora to stop.

Mattie was inching over to John's pistol when Zora heard Mrs. G----, one of Mattie's few friends, coming to help. Zora reached a hatchet leaning against a wall just as Mrs. G---- came through the doorway. Zora flung the hatchet, and the blade banged into the wall near Mrs. G----'s head. Mrs. G---- left.

Mattie was limp from Zora's beating when John Hurston, weeping, stepped in and pulled Zora off. He saved his wife, after a fashion, but he couldn't save their marriage.

Mattie told John he had to have Zora arrested. But the only things he *had* to do were die and stay black. He wouldn't send his daughter to jail.

So Mattie tried to get the church to step in and do something, anything. The church members laughed at her. After months of wrangling, Mattie Hurston left her husband and Eatonville. She would come back when John decided to stick up for her. Mattie never came back. Zora had been the last straw.

so long, eatonville

Zora's memories of Eatonville hurt like anything now, so she headed for another town to find a job. She didn't turn up any work right away. But she did find a collection of John Milton's poetry in a rubbish pile, and she soaked it up like a sponge. Zora's spirits badly needed a boost, and Milton's rhymes and rhythms did the trick.

Then her brother Bob asked her to come live with him and his family in Memphis, Tennessee. He had just graduated from medical school, and he wanted to help send Zora to school too.

Zora thought her prayers had been answered. She could go to school again! She would have a home. "My five haunted years were over!" she wrote. "I said goodbye—not to anybody in particular, but to the town, to loneliness, to defeat and frustration, to shabby living, to sterile houses and numbed pangs, to the kind of people I had no wish to know; to an era."

When Zora got to Bob's place, he explained that he couldn't send her to school right away after all. If he did, his wife would say he was pampering Zora. Zora should work around the house for a spell—until he could think of a way to get her in school without annoying his wife.

Zora wanted badly to finish high school, but she just couldn't, at least not right then. So she devoted herself to Bob's children. She told them stories and bided her time.

Bob's children, Wilhemina (top left), Winifred (bottom center), and Edgar (right) heard many a good story when their aunt Zora took care of them.

While she lived with Bob's family, Zora became friends with a neighbor who told her about a job—a singer in a traveling show needed a lady's maid. Zora's friend was a poor white woman, but she bought Zora a new navy blue dress with a round, white collar for her job interview. Zora loved hats, so Valena, the woman's daughter, lent her one. Zora thought she had never looked so pretty before. Her friend gave Zora carfare, and all the advice she had.

The singer, Miss M----, liked Zora and hired her at $10 a week. Miss M---- thought Zora was fifteen years old; she was actually twenty-four. Imagine that.

Zora didn't know what Bob would say about her new job. She wasn't taking any chances though. Just in case Bob wouldn't let her take the job, Zora never went back to his house. She stayed with her friend instead.

At the end of the week, the show was moving on, and Zora with it. Zora didn't have a suitcase, so Miss M---- advanced her enough money to buy one. With her first week's pay, Zora paid her friend back for her dress. Then she bought a toothbrush, toothpaste, a comb and brush, and two handkerchiefs. Valena gave Zora extra underpants, stockings, and the interview hat. Zora stuffed her new suitcase with crumpled newspapers to keep her few things from rattling around.

Zora was enchanted by the show company. The glamour, the elegance, the music dazzled her. She listened to the operettas the cast performed and learned to love them. Once, while listening to a duet from the stage's wings, Zora thought, "If there [is] any more to

Heaven than this, I [don't] want to see it."

As the only African American in the theater company, Zora was a center of attention and the butt of many good-natured jokes. Zora easily drawled her way into the good graces of those show people, mostly Northerners.

Before long, her new maid was spending so much time with the other cast members that Miss M---- put a stop to Zora's late-night talk sessions. Miss M---- wanted Zora all to herself.

Zora could always sniff out a book, and the company's tenor agreed to let her read some of his. Zora wanted to go to school again more than ever.

Zora's writing career began accidentally. The performers had given her pictures of themselves to put in a scrapbook, and Zora wrote comments under each picture. Egged on by the company, and no doubt pleased by all the fuss being made over her, Zora started to post her daily comments on a bulletin board. Now everyone could read them. Zora was a writer.

When the tour was over, Zora went to Miss M----'s home in Boston, and then went with her on her next touring job. While on this next trip, Miss M---- met and fell in love with a man who proposed marriage. Miss M---- accepted.

Miss M---- planned to leave the stage after her marriage, so she would no longer need a maid. When the company got to Baltimore, Miss M---- gave Zora a little money, and that was that. Zora was out of a job in a strange city.

Somehow Zora persuaded a restaurant owner to hire her as a waitress. She didn't pay enough attention to be good at the job though. Her mind wandered. On top of that, if the women weren't looking down their noses at her, the men were trying to hit on her. Zora couldn't stand being groped *and* disrespected. She soon got fired.

As if things weren't bad enough, Zora suffered an attack of appendicitis. She had no money, so she had to go to the free ward at Maryland General Hospital. On the way to the operating room, Zora made a deal with God. She promised that if she lived through the surgery, she would truly follow whatever direction in life seemed to be the right one. She would do whatever God wanted her to do. Whether she kept her promise is Zora's secret.

school at last

Zora wanted to go to school! She had no money for tuition, but so what? "I just went," she later wrote.

Baltimore's night high school was free, and that's where Zora started. Her teacher, an African American named Dwight O. W. Holmes, cheered and encouraged her to no end.

The fire in Dwight Holmes's eyes lit up the poetry of Samuel Taylor Coleridge. When Holmes glanced up from the page, he looked straight at Zora. For her, Coleridge's words became images. For days afterward, she was "not of the work-a-day world."

Inspired by Holmes, Zora quit night school to register at Morgan Academy, the high-school department of Morgan College. Morgan was a school for African Americans.

Direct as usual, Zora simply went to the college in September 1917 and asked to talk to the dean. The dean, William Pickens, was a colored man. He understood her situation. He accepted her as a student and gave her credit for two years of high school. Mrs. Pickens found a job for Zora—helping the bedridden wife of a local minister.

As part of her job, Zora had to live with Reverend Baldwin and his family. That was all right with Zora, because she needed a place to stay anyway. The Baldwins' large library was more than all right. It was wonderful.

Zora had a powerful hunger for words. She memorized poems, in case she never got another chance to read them. Zora was twenty-six years old and starting to get an education.

When classes began at Morgan Academy, Zora had one pair of shoes, one dress, and one change of underwear. Her well-off, well-dressed classmates liked her just the same. They were the sons and daughters of lawyers and doctors and such. Zora, "in the middle of all this pretty," felt that her face "had been chopped out of a knot of pine wood with a hatchet on somebody's off day."

Zora loved Morgan Academy: "I was at last doing the things I wanted to do. Every new thing I learned in school made me happy." In the subjects she liked, Zora excelled. She was even sometimes put in charge of her English and history classes. She talked so well, she won a prize in a speech-making contest.

During Zora's first year at Morgan, John Hurston died in an automobile accident. "We were all so sorry for him, instead of being bitter," Zora wrote. "Old Maker had left out the steering gear when He gave Papa his talents. . . . With my mother gone and nobody to guide him, life . . . had turned him loose to hurt himself."

Zora had planned to attend Morgan College after graduating from the academy, but a chance meeting with a Howard University student changed all that. Mae Miller felt certain that Zora was "Howard material" and urged her to apply. A friend of Zora's from Morgan Academy offered to let her stay at her family's home in Washington, D.C. That way, Zora wouldn't have to pay for a room. Zora was sure to find a job to help pay tuition.

Howard was the biggest and most famous African-American college in the country. To Zora, it was "the capstone of Negro education in the world." She thought Howard might even be too hard for her, that she wouldn't succeed. Maybe then she heard Lucy's words again. Anyway, she went for what she really wanted—Howard University. Zora jumped at the sun.

The Old Main building of Howard University, in Washington, D.C. Zora wanted to "be worthy to stand there under the shadow of the hovering spirit of Howard. I felt the ladder under my feet."

That summer of 1918, Zora moved to Washington. She worked briefly as a waitress, and then as a manicurist in a barber shop. She started filling in the gaps in her schooling at Howard's preparatory high school. There she met Herbert Sheen of Decatur, Illinois, who was working his way through Howard as a waiter. Zora fell in love—flat out and grinning from ear to ear. She wrote, "He could stomp a piano out of this world, sing a fair baritone and dance beautifully. . . . For the first time since my mother's death, there was someone who felt really close and warm to me."

Zora and Herbert went together for over a year, even after he left Washington for New York, and then left New York for medical school in Chicago. Zora and Herbert had to settle for love letters for the time being.

Broke as usual, Zora scuffled along, going to classes, studying, and working in low-paying jobs. She sometimes worked as a maid for wealthy colored families. When she ran out of money, she borrowed from friends. During this time, Zora also suffered a serious, and unknown, illness. It was perhaps the beginning of the intestinal trouble that would plague her all her life.

Zora kept plugging and got an associate degree from Howard Academy in 1920. She started at Howard University the same year.

Zora was much taken with Howard, her teachers, her friends, and college life in general. She was fascinated by all those polished, well-educated colored people. Howard was the last word.

Zora (center) with two of her classmates at Howard. She worked hard to keep up with her studies and pay her way. The result was *A*'s in the courses she liked and *F*'s in the courses she hated (Physical Education was one of these).

Alain Locke was a young philosophy professor at Howard University when Zora went there. A graduate of Harvard, he was the first African-American Rhodes scholar and a brilliant literary critic dedicated to encouraging black writers.

The teachers at Howard University urged Zora to write. So she did. Zora used folktales she had heard in Eatonville as part of "John Redding Goes to Sea." The story won the yearly contest of the Stylus, a college literary society formed by Howard professor Alain Leroy Locke. It was published in the club's magazine in 1921—when Zora was thirty, passing for perhaps twenty.

Charles Spurgeon Johnson read "John Redding..." in the Stylus's magazine. Charles Johnson worked for the National Urban League, which helped African Americans from the South adjust to life in large northern cities. Johnson edited *Opportunity: A Journal of Negro Life,* the league's magazine, and he was always looking for black talent. He thought that if African-American writers and artists showed their African genius, then white people would no longer feel superior to them. Charles Johnson was a dreamer.

Johnson liked "John Redding . . .," and he asked Zora to send something to *Opportunity.* Near the end of 1924, Zora submitted "Drenched in Light," a story about a little girl who swings on her garden gate. Johnson published it.

During his long career as a sociologist and teacher, Charles S. Johnson did as much to promote black creative talent as anybody ever has. Many historians say that he was the prime mover behind what became known as the *Harlem Renaissance.* Johnson later became the first black president of Fisk University.

A better writer than student, Zora finally left Howard University in 1924 without graduating. She had missed a lot of classes because of illness and because she had to work to support herself. Studying always had to take a back seat.

In 1925, Alain Locke chose another of Zora's stories, "Spunk," to include in *The New Negro*—a special issue of *Survey Graphic* magazine. Encouraged by her success, Zora submitted "Spunk" and a play, *Color Struck,* to *Opportunity's* first literary contest.

Each work won a prize, and Zora was invited to the awards dinner in New York City in May. She got there "with $1.50, no job, no friends, and a lot of hope." At the dinner, Zora met two other award-winning young writers—Countee Cullen and Langston Hughes.

The 1920s were a rich period in the arts of African America. Books, essays, short stories, paintings, sculpture, and music by African Americans were all the rage. Most of all, as Langston Hughes said, "the Negro was in vogue."

During the Roaring Twenties, white and black people alike came to see African Americans in plays, musicals, concerts, cabarets, jazz combos, art exhibits, and literary readings.

Harlem, a black section of New York City, was the biggest African-American neighborhood in the country. White New Yorkers hung out in Harlem, seeing and being seen. White organizations sought African-American artists to give money to. Theatergoers queued up for anything with or about African Americans. Zora was a part of this Negro Renaissance, later called the Harlem Renaissance, or the Black Renaissance.

"Sp_nk" caught the attention of Fannie Hurst, a well-known white novelist and a judge of the *Opportunity* contest. Hurst hired Zora as her live-in secretary. But the details of typing and filing didn't suit Zora at all. Hurst fired her.

Flamboyant and spoiled, Fanny Hurst once introduced Zora as an African princess so Zora could come with her into a "whites-only" restaurant. Zora found the dinner "bitter." This photo was taken of Hurst in 1911.

Fannie liked Zora, though, so she rehired her to drive her car and keep her company. Zora told a friend that Fannie liked having her around because Zora's brown skin complemented Fannie's paleness. She said that Fannie "amazed me with her moods."

At the *Opportunity* awards dinner, Zora had been noticed by another influential white woman. Annie Nathan Meyer had helped found Barnard College, the women's division of Columbia University, in New York City. Annie Meyer arranged for Zora to get a scholarship to Barnard, beginning in the autumn of 1925. School!

Zora in New York City

Zora called herself "Barnard's sacred black cow." *Everybody* wanted to be Zora's friend. She was a published author, the only African American at Barnard, and she worked for a best-selling novelist. Zora was so popular with the other students that she ran into little obvious racism. Zora was in vogue.

Zora's apartment in Harlem became a gathering place for writers, artists, and musicians. With a steady income, Zora was always good for a meal, a kind word, or a place to crash. Her eavesdropping at Joe Clarke's store was starting to pay off—Zora could tell funny stories as well as anybody. When she was talking, she was the center of attention. And Zora *loved* being the center of attention.

One story Zora probably told was this:

> *Sewell is a man who lives all to himself. He moves a great deal. So often, that 'Lige Moseley says his chickens are so used to moving that every time he comes out into his backyard the chickens lie down and cross their legs, ready to be tied up again.*
>
> *He is baldheaded; but he says he doesn't mind . . . because he wants as little as possible between him and God.*

There were plenty of good times in Harlem. But the demands of being a full-time student were wearing on Zora. She wrote to Countee Cullen, "The regular grind at Barnard is beginning to drive me lopsided. . . . I hate routine."

Nonetheless, Zora stuck it out to the end of the year. In Barnard's "Record of Freshman Interest," Zora wrote, "I have had some small success as a writer and wish above all to succeed at it." That wish never changed.

poking and prying

In the summer of 1926, Zora joined writers Wallace Thurman, Langston Hughes, Bruce Nugent, and Gwendolyn Bennett; and artist Aaron Douglas in organizing *Fire!!,* — a quarterly magazine of African-American literature.

In part, *Fire!!* was a reaction to Charles Johnson and W. E. B. Du Bois, editor of *The Crisis,* the magazine of the National Association for the Advancement of Colored People. Du Bois and Johnson wanted to use African-American literature and art to show white people what African Americans were really like. The *Fire!!* group felt that trying to change white people's opinions gave white people too much attention. Zora, Wallace, and the others wanted "more outlets for Negro fire," whether white people thought well of them or not.

The *Fire!!* writers needed white people's support as much as anybody. They just didn't want to act like it.

After the contributors chipped in to get *Fire!!* published, most of the printed copies were destroyed by a real fire. Since there were no magazines to sell, the creditors couldn't be paid. *Fire!!* went out after only one issue.

Zora's disappointment was balanced by a new interest. In her first year at Barnard, Zora had discovered anthropology—the study of people and their cultures. And Franz Boas, the nation's leading anthropologist, had discovered Zora. Elderly, German-born Boas had taken Zora under his wing, encouraging her to study folklore—stories, customs, sayings, and art forms that a community tells and retells to each other. The "spyglass of anthropology" had shown Zora that Eatonville's storytelling was as creative as anything European. For Zora Hurston, nothing would ever be the same.

As a young man, Dr. Franz Boas made a great name for himself studying many undocumented cultures. He considered all cultural traditions equal. Zora thought that Dr. Boas was the "greatest anthropologist alive," calling him "Papa Franz" to his face and "king of kings" behind his back. Through his training, Zora was invited to be a member of the American Folk-Lore Society, American Ethnological Society, and the American Anthropological Society.

In February 1927, Zora took a train south to do what she called "poking and prying with a purpose." Zora was going to record the folklore of African Americans in the Florida countryside. Zora's "Papa Franz" was in charge of the project. The Association for the Study of Negro Life and History, led by historian Carter Godwin Woodson, was footing the bill. After borrowing money for an old car to get around in, Zora set out on her first collecting trip.

African-American folklore was just beginning to be studied seriously in the United States. Zora had a chance to break new ground, and she blew it.

Back in Eatonville and other black communities in the South, Zora felt very much the professional and very full of herself. She was pompous and snooty. Her highfalutin manner put people off. "Oh, I got a few little items. But compared with what I did later, not enough to make a flea a waltzing jacket," she wrote. "I needed my Barnard education to help me see my people as they really are. But I found that it did not do to be too detached. . . . I had to go back, dress as they did, talk as they did, live their life, so that I could get into my stories the world I knew as a child."

The collecting hadn't gone well, but the trip wasn't a total loss. Zora had arranged to meet Herbert Sheen in May. Zora and Herbert had been carrying on their long-distance romance for nearly eight years. Their time had come.

Yet Zora had doubts about the match from the start. The night before Herbert arrived in St. Augustine, Zora dreamed that "a dark shadow kept falling between us. . . . It was as vivid as noon." Just the same, Herbert and Zora were wed on May 19, 1927.

Soon after the wedding, Zora was anxious to get on with her research and writing. But Herbert wanted a wife, not a folklorist.

She wrote later, "I asked myself if I were in love, or if this had been a habit. . . . Somebody had turned a hose on the sun. What I had taken for eternity turned out to be a moment walking in its sleep." Zora and Herbert's marriage fizzled after only a few months.

Hoping to end things neatly, Zora encouraged Herbert to return to medical school. He did. Herbert later lamented, "The demands of her career doomed the marriage to an early, amicable divorce." Since neither of them could afford to pay for it, their divorce was more amicable than early. They were actually married for four years altogether. Zora and Herbert were still friendly twenty-five years later, when Zora wrote, "Your own mother has never loved you to the depth I have, Herbert."

Alone again, Zora set out for Mobile, Alabama, to interview Kossola-O-Lo-Loo-Ay, also called Cudjo Lewis. Kossola was the last survivor of the last ship that brought African slaves to the United States. Probably bored with the details of field research and perhaps frustrated because interviewing the eighty-year-old ex-slave was so hard, Zora copied someone else's work.

Zora eventually turned in an article on Kossola for the *Journal of Negro History* that was sixty-seven paragraphs long. Zora wrote eighteen of them herself and stole the rest from *Historic Sketches of the Old South,* by Emma Langdon Roche. Nobody knew that Zora had copied Roche's work until 1972. Zora's reasons for the plagiarism remain unknown.

Kossola and his great-great grandchildren in 1927

Making the most of having a car, Zora visited her brothers Bob and Ben in Memphis, Tennessee. Bob and Zora hadn't seen each other since she had gone off to work for Miss M----. Bob's medical practice was coming along well, and Ben owned the East Memphis Drug Store. As for the rest of the Hurstons, Clifford was the principal of the Negro high school in Decatur, Alabama. Dick was drifting up and down the East Coast, making his way as a chef. John owned a grocery market in Jacksonville, Florida. Everette, the youngest, worked for the post office in Brooklyn, New York. Sarah was still married to a man "for whom [the family] all wished a short sickness and a quick funeral."

After leaving Bob and Ben, Zora ran across her pal Langston Hughes in Mobile, Alabama. Langston was at loose ends, and the two of them headed north together in Zora's jalopy. They collected folklore along the way and even stopped in Macon, Georgia, to hear Bessie Smith sing.

Back in New York in September, Zora met Mrs. Rufus Osgood Mason. Alain Locke probably introduced them. Charlotte Louise van der Veer Quick Mason was a rich, white widow with a soft spot in her purse for African Americans. She gave money to several black artists and writers, including Langston Hughes and Alain Locke.

As soon as she saw Charlotte, Zora knew she was someone from her childhood visions. Zora even recognized the flowers in Charlotte's apartment as the strange white flowers she had seen in one of the scenes.

Charlotte Mason had a longstanding interest in anthropology. As a young woman, she had spent months living among Native American peoples on the plains, sponsoring an anthropologist to study their cultures. Though she was elderly in the 1920s, Langston Hughes wrote that Godmother was "an amazing, brilliant personality."

A kind racist, Charlotte Mason thought that African people were charming but primitive. If they seemed otherwise, they weren't being "authentic." Mason didn't think much of Locke's obvious European refinement. He acted too white.

Chock-full of Eatonville sayings and with a drawl thick as blackstrap molasses, Zora didn't act at all like white people. She and Charlotte got on famously and could even read each other's mind.

But at Charlotte's Manhattan apartment, Zora sometimes faced criticism from Charlotte and Charlotte's friends. Then Zora felt "like a rabbit at a dog convention." Charlotte felt she had a right to criticize Zora because she had become Zora's patron, or source of money. She would pay Zora to collect African-American folklore, because she couldn't do it herself. In return, Charlotte insisted on being called "Godmother", and that's what Zora called her.

For a struggling folklorist with no advanced degree, Godmother was a godsend. Zora could finally do just what she wanted. She didn't have to think about making a living. From Godmother, Zora got $200 a month, a movie camera, and "Sassy Susie" (a car). In exchange, Godmother owned the rights to everything Zora discovered and everything Zora wrote.

In December 1927, Zora became the first African-American woman to graduate from Barnard. Then, with Godmother's money, she headed for Mobile, Alabama, and Kossola again.

Zora wrote up her second interview with Kossola as a story—art, not anthropology. Zora wanted to *use* the folklore she collected, not just record it.

Florida came next. In late January 1928, Zora pulled into a lumber and turpentine camp in Polk County, Florida. The workers in the camp were her people. Everybody's heritage was African except the boss's.

Remembering her failure at collecting folklore in Eatonville, Zora tried to blend in this time. Although she never drank, Zora told the Polk County workers she was a bootlegger's woman. Folks expected bootleggers—people who sell illegal alcohol—to have plenty of money. That explained Zora's car and slick clothes.

Zora made friends with Big Sweet, the toughest woman around. Big Sweet knew who had good stories and songs, and she made them tell Zora. Big Sweet helped set up storytelling contests and judged them herself. Nobody argued about the results.

Zora takes a sassy pose in front of her car, "Sassy Susie." After her narrow escape in Polk County, Zora began carrying a pistol whenever she went collecting folklore.

One of the people Zora interviewed in Polk County was Slim, Lucy's man. Lucy was going for bad, and she didn't like Zora talking to Slim one bit. Lucy wanted to make a reputation for herself, and she spread the word that she was out to do Zora in. Frightened, Zora began going nowhere without Big Sweet.

By and by, Lucy found Zora in a jook joint—a nightclub in the country for colored people. Zora was scared witless. She just stood there, numb.

As Lucy charged at Zora with a knife, Big Sweet charged at Lucy. Zora charged for the door. Big Sweet called out to Zora, "Run!" Zora ran. "When the sun came up," she wrote, "I was a hundred miles up the road, headed for New Orleans."

In New Orleans, Louisiana, Zora studied hoodoo—traditional African beliefs mixed with Roman Catholicism. She became an apprentice to a hoodoo expert so she could learn the arts of the faith. By September,

Zora had learned eighteen tasks, including how to kill. She earned the "Crown of Power" by lying on a couch for sixty-nine hours. She was naked all that time, with her navel touching a snakeskin.

"I knew that I had been accepted [by the spirits] before the sixty-nine hours had passed," she wrote. "I had five psychic experiences."

In late April 1929, Zora rented a little cabin in Eau Gallie, Florida, to organize her field notes. She felt that hoodoo conjurers had discovered many secrets of nature. To her, hoodoo was no more primitive than Catholicism. She knew, though, that her conclusions would shock and offend many people, so she wrote to Papa Franz for his advice. Boas warned Zora about stirring up controversy. But he failed to discourage her. Stubborn, Zora included an account of her hoodoo research in her manuscript on Florida folklore, *Mules and Men.*

A hoodoo conjurer lounges on her stoop in New Orleans. This sketch and the sketch of a hoodoo ceremony on the next page were done in the late 1800s by Edward Windsor Kemble.

In August 1929, Zora turned up in southern Florida, collecting African-American songs and stories around Miami. Then she briefly recorded folklore in the Bahamas before going back to New Orleans in October.

Zora told Godmother she was doing more hoodoo research. Actually, she was working in secret with anthropologist Otto Klineberg. Zora had told Godmother earlier that she wanted to work with Klineberg, but Godmother had flatly refused to allow it. Zora's manuscript of *Mules and Men* was in Godmother's safe-deposit box. So if Zora wanted to get her work published, she had to toe Godmother's line, or at least make her *think* she was toeing her line. Godmother liked having her own personal folklorist, and she wasn't *about* to give up her control.

At thirty-eight years old, Zora couldn't publish *anything,* even fiction, without Godmother's approval. Zora didn't like it, but she needed the money. So she sent some of her notes from New Orleans to Langston, and wrote wistfully, "I hope you can use them."

zora plays

In early 1930, Godmother set Zora up in an apartment in Westfield, New Jersey, so Zora could concentrate on writing. Langston, who was also on Godmother's payroll, lived nearby.

Zora and Langston had talked about working together on a stage production. With Godmother's support, they began to write a comedy in three acts, based on one of Zora's folktales. Godmother hired Louise Thompson, a former teacher, to be their secretary.

As she typed, Louise offered suggestions. Langston liked Louise's ideas. Zora resented Louise's interference. Langston thought Louise should share credit for the play, entitled *Mule Bone*. Zora later wrote him, "Now Langston, nobody has in the history of the world given a typist an interest in a work for typing it. Nobody would think of it unless they were prejudiced in favor of the typist."

Zora simmered for several weeks, uncharacteristically keeping her mouth shut. She must have liked Langston a lot. She left New Jersey in May, heading south for the summer. Still, she apparently planned to complete Act II over the summer.

In September, Zora returned to New Jersey and ended her silence. She told Langston that she had no time for him. By December, she was refusing to see him. Zora wanted to get *Mule Bone* produced as her own. Most of the material was from her collecting trips, and she felt a right of ownership.

Langston Hughes and Zora Neale Hurston. Langston wrote of her: "Only to reach a wider audience, need she ever write books—because she is a perfect book of entertainment in herself . . . . She could make you laugh one minute and cry the next." This photograph of Zora was taken by her friend Carl Van Vechten the fall of 1931.

Zora let Carl Van Vechten—a well-known white novelist, critic, and supporter of black artists—read *Mule Bone.* Without telling Zora, Van Vechten sent the manuscript to Barrett Clark, a reader for the Theatre Guild, who sent it to Rowena Jellife, a director of Karamu House in Cleveland, Ohio. Karamu House was the home of the Gilpin Players, an African-American acting company.

In January 1931, Langston was recovering from an illness at his mother's home in Cleveland. He had cut his ties with Godmother. His friend Rowena Jellife showed him a play the Gilpin Players wanted to perform. The play was *Mule Bone*—by Zora Neale Hurston. Why wasn't Langston listed as coauthor? Langston tried to get Zora by phone, but couldn't. Zora didn't answer his letters either. So Langston called Arthur Spingarn, his attorney, to see what he could do. Over the next couple of weeks, Zora, Langston, Spingarn, and Carl Van Vechten traded letters, telegrams, and spoken words, trying to work things out.

Zora came to Cleveland on the first of February for a meeting with Langston. No one knows what they said to each other, but the two of them agreed to let the Gilpin Players do the play. Just when it seemed that *Mule Bone* would at last be produced, Zora found out that Louise had recently been to see Langston.

Louise had come to Cleveland for her own work— not about *Mule Bone.* But Zora thought she was being double-crossed and pitched a fit.

Zora stormed over to Langston's mother's house, where

she ranted about Langston, his mother, the Gilpin Players, and Rowena Jellife. *Mule Bone* was abandoned, and Zora left for New York. Zora Hurston and Langston Hughes had been the best of friends; they were friends no more.

During this time, Zora was still trying to pound her field notes into a form that someone would publish. She had been working steadily and had submitted the manuscripts of *Mules and Men* and other works to several New York publishers.

Zora often visited her youngest brother Everette in Brooklyn, New York. His son, Everette, Jr., romps in Aunt Zora's Chevy in 1931.

The rejection slips were piling up. Godmother was losing patience. She canceled Zora's contract at the end of March 1931. Zora no longer had a steady income.

By summer, Zora was broke. She even thought about selling fried chicken to make money. Godmother broke down and gave her $100 for the month of June. But Zora needed more, and she needed it regularly. She scraped by.

Zora still wanted to present folktales on the stage. She got a chance when a white producer asked her to contribute to a show he was putting together. That summer, she began writing three sketches for *Fast and Furious.* The humor in the rest of the show was stale and used insulting images of African people. Zora said that the producer was "stupid and trite." He "squeezed all Negro-ness out of everything and substituted what he thought... to be Negro humor."

But times were hard. The Great Depression lay across the United States, and millions of people were out of work. The Negro was no longer in vogue. So Zora finished her work for the show and even performed in it with Jackie (later "Moms") Mabley. *Fast and Furious* was dreadful, and it closed after one week. Zora made $75.

Before Godmother would give Zora any more money, she made Zora list her expenses. Zora painstakingly detailed her purchases, down to colon medicine for her stomach pain and canned fruit.

In the fall of 1931, Zora's luck began to change. Nancy Cunard—rich, white, and British—was putting together a collection of writings by African Americans. She asked Zora to contribute some folklore. Zora wrote essays about the ways that African people make art out of the spoken word. She said that African Americans had "the will to adorn." Their talk was rich and vivid.

Zora felt that white people were culturally deprived because their speech was flat and dull. Black figures of speech had "done wonders to the English language."

Disgusted by *Fast and Furious,* Zora decided to produce her own show about African Americans. She collected her own performers. She used her own material, and she rehearsed in her own apartment. She didn't have her own money, though, so she wrote to Godmother, "I have . . . worked so hard to get [my play] into shape, [that] I am willing to make any sacrifice, meet any terms to give it a chance of success." Zora had already pawned her radio and sold her car when Godmother came through. She backed Zora's show, *The Great Day,* for one grand New York performance, on January 10, 1932.

The New York performance of *The Great Day* in 1932 was a smashing success. It was so successful that it was later invited to the National Folklore Festival in St. Louis. In this promotional photograph, Zora can be seen on the far right.

The Great Day portrayed a day in a railway camp with work songs, a sermon, spirituals, and blues at a jook joint. Zora had originally ended it with a hoodoo conjure ceremony, but Godmother would only let her present that material in a book. Godmother thought the stage would make hoodoo look cheap.

The Great Day got good reviews, and the New York *Herald Tribune* wanted it to keep playing. Zora rejoiced that, "the world wanted to hear the glorious voice of my people."

Unfortunately, Zora was a truly awful businesswoman. After paying the theater rental, she didn't have enough money left to pay the cast. Godmother paid them off and had her lawyer draw up papers making it clear that Zora had to repay the entire $610 she owed her for *The Great Day*. Later that month, Zora got more papers from Godmother's lawyer that listed the parts of *The Great Day* that Zora could stage to make money. Anything else could "not be used for any purpose without further permission from [Godmother]."

Zora went along with Godmother's program. She staged only the Godmother-approved parts of *The Great Day,* while she tried to get a book published. She put on performances wherever she could make a few dollars.

Zora was broke, and now she was homesick. In April, Godmother reluctantly bought Zora a ticket to Eatonville and gave her enough cash to replace her only pair of shoes. Zora stayed with her friends the Moseleys and relaxed in the warmth of Eatonville.

In the autumn of 1932, Zora got together an Eatonville

cast for a January 1933 performance of *The Great Day* at nearby Rollins College. To ease the pain in her intestines, she directed some rehearsals sitting on an inner tube.

Now called *From Sun to Sun,* her show was a hit again. But Zora still wasn't making a living. Whatever she got from the occasional one-day shows just wasn't enough. To earn some money, Zora wrote "The Gilded Six-Bits." This short story was published in *Story* magazine's August issue. After reading it, publisher Bertram Lippincott asked Zora if she was working on a novel. She wasn't, but she said she was.

travel dust

Zora wrote *Jonah's Gourd Vine* on grit. She knew there would be too many distractions in Eatonville, so she rented a one-room house in Sanford, Florida, for $1.50 a week. Every Friday, a cousin lent her $.50 for food. She got the manuscript typed on credit and borrowed $1.83 to mail it. By the time she finished in early September, Zora owed $18.00 in back rent.

Zora and the cast members of *From Sun to Sun* were scheduled to put on a show in Sanford's business district on October 16, 1933. Zora expected to earn $25 for herself, and she promised her landlady that she would pay what she owed. The landlady didn't believe Zora would *ever* have that much money. She evicted Zora on the spot. With no place else to go, Zora shifted her clothes and the card table she worked on to her uncle Isaiah's. Then she set out to entertain the citizens of Sanford.

Zora was riding on a sound truck with her singers when she got a telegram. She was busy, so she put it in her pocket until later. After the show, she went to a shoe store with the gift certificate the chamber of commerce had given her. Zora always needed shoes, and she was trying some on when she remembered the telegram.

J. B. Lippincott Company wanted to publish *Jonah's Gourd Vine*. Would she accept an advance of $200? Zora ran all the way to the Western Union office wearing one new shoe and one old one. She wrote later, "I never expect to have a greater thrill than that wire gave me. You know the feeling when you found your first pubic hair. Greater than that."

Zora staged *From Sun to Sun* here and there in Florida. The audiences were segregated, but at least she was earning a little money. *From Sun to Sun* caught the attention of Mary McLeod Bethune, the African-American president of Bethune-Cookman College in Daytona Beach, Florida. She was much impressed by the production and asked Zora to set up a school of dramatic arts at Bethune-Cookman. Zora arrived in Daytona Beach in January 1934, ready to build a school "based on pure Negro expression."

But Zora didn't take kindly to rules, and Bethune-Cookman had a *lot* of rules. Zora said she had trouble even getting a light bulb for her office. By April 1934, Zora had given up on "the farce of Bethune-Cookman's Drama Department."

In May, *Jonah's Gourd Vine* hit the bookstores. Zora

was a published novelist. Lippincott now wanted to publish her folklore. Zora spent the summer in a cabin in the woods near Loughman, Florida, fine-tuning *Mules and Men* and writing fiction on the side.

Some of Zora's race felt that much of her work was "primitive," because it was so *different*. It wasn't "refined" from a European point of view. Angered and frustrated, Zora wrote that trying to be like white people was "the intellectual lynching we [African Americans] perpetrate upon ourselves. . . . Roll your eyes in ecstasy and ape [a white man's] every move, but until we have placed something upon his street corner that is our own, we are right back where we were when they filed our iron collar [of slavery] off."

Zora knew that black art was as good as anything white. She explained, "You see, no matter how much talent a Negro may have, if he is sent to a white [school] he is ruined. . . . He loses the flavor and quality that sets him apart from white artists. . . . This native quality [should] be increased rather than obliterated."

Zora would mimic, dance, and cut capers. Here she is teaching some friends a West African Crow Dance.

Zora renamed her show again and presented *Singing Steel* to an audience of steelworkers in Chicago. Afterward, representatives of the Julius Rosenwald Foundation offered Zora a fellowship to study for a Ph.D. back at Columbia University. Zora decided to go for the advanced degree. Then more people would take her work seriously.

She and Papa Franz drew up a study plan. Zora intended to do her field study after three semesters of graduate school. Edwin Embree, president of the foundation, wanted her to have more class time. He wanted to "transform . . . the brilliant Miss Hurston" into a bookworm. Embree refused long-term support.

Zora had been counting on the foundation's money and was depressed at being treated so shabbily. She said, "My mental state was such that I could neither think nor plan. . . . I had got to the place I was talking to myself."

Zora accepted Embree's conditions, although she probably never intended to stick to them. She stayed at Columbia long enough to ensure that she would get the $100-a-month payments. Then she ignored school and worked on her own, writing. This was a tough time for Zora, because her school plans and her love life were going sour at the same time.

Zora had been seeing a man she called A. W. P. off and on since they'd met in 1931. Back then, he had been a graduate student at Columbia University. He was only twenty-three years old and bashful. They didn't spend much time together at first. Both of them were afraid of being hurt, afraid to declare themselves.

Then A.W. P. began paying her compliments. At his Alpha Phi Alpha fraternity dance, A.W. P. told her how he wanted to clothe her in "a gorgeous evening wrap and everything to go with it." Zora was smitten.

"He was tall, dark brown, magnificently built," she wrote. "But his looks only drew my eyes in the beginning. I did not fall in love with him just for that. He had a fine mind and that intrigued me. When a man keeps beating me to the draw mentally, he begins to get glamorous. I did not just fall in love. I made a parachute jump."

But as with Herbert, "He begged me to give up my career, marry him and live outside of New York City. I really wanted to do anything he wanted me to do, but that one thing I could not do. . . . I had things clawing inside of me that must be said. . . . He felt that he did not matter to me enough. . . . [It had to be] All, or nothing, for him."

Zora was jealous of other women and afraid that one would win A.W. P.'s heart. "I hated to think of him smiling unless he was smiling at me," she wrote. "His grins were too precious to be wasted on ordinary mortals, especially women."

Eventually, Zora's temper got the better of her. In the heat of an argument, she slapped him. He exploded and hit her back. She wrote, "I realized afterwards that my hot head could tell me to beat him, but it would cost me something. I would have to bring head to get head. . . . Then I knew I was too deeply in love to be my old self. For always a blow to my body had infuriated me beyond measure. . . . But somehow, I didn't hate him at all." She later called their relationship "the real love affair of my life." Zora and A.W. P. went on arguing and making up and getting nowhere.

Zora lived on the Rosenwald grant for the first half of 1935. She wrote Embree in June that the money had been well spent, although not on graduate school. Instead, she had written two plays and the first draft of a new novel.

Zora hadn't yet made up her mind what to do about her relationship with A.W. P. She thought that getting away from him would clear her head and help her decide what to do. So in the summer of 1935, Zora went to Florida to do research with white folklorists Mary Elizabeth Barnicle and Alan Lomax.

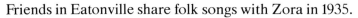

Friends in Eatonville share folk songs with Zora in 1935.

Zora led Lomax and Barnicle to backwoods villages to record the customs, songs, and stories of African Americans. Black people and white people weren't allowed to hang out socially. Zora got Lomax and Barnicle to blacken their faces, so the white police wouldn't notice them.

Zora and Mary Barnicle eventually quarreled. Alan Lomax put the disagreement down to "some woman thing." He added, "They always had professional respect for each other." Zora stayed behind in Florida to work on her own, and the rest of the team went on without her. Lomax, at least, was sorry that Zora stayed behind. "To watch her work was a revelation to me," he said. In his opinion, Zora was "probably the best informed person today on Western Negro folklore."

Mules and Men was published in October 1935. It was the first book of African-American folklore written by an African American. Some stories had truth to them; some were just tall tales told for the fun of it. White reviewers liked the study as entertainment. Here's why:

> *You know, when it lightnings, de angels is peepin' in de lookin' glass; when it thunders, they's rollin' out de rain barrels; and when it rains, somebody done dropped a barrel or two and bust it.*
>
> *One time . . . ,there was going to be big doin's in Glory and all de angels had brand new clothes . . . and so they was all peepin' in the lookin' glasses, and . . . it got to lightning all over. . . . God tole some of de angels to roll in all de full rain barrels and they was in such a hurry that it was thunderin' from the east to the west and . . . some of them angels . . . dropped a whole heap of them rain barrels, and didn't it rain!*

Poverty and prejudice were the two *P*s that most black people in the early 1900s knew well. Thus most influential African Americans felt it was the responsibility of all black writers to write about these things. Zora responded, "I am not tragically colored. There is no great sorrow dammed up in my soul . . . . I do not belong to the sobbing school of Negrohood."

Many African Americans complained that the book didn't show how angry they were. Poet Sterling Brown said, "*Mules and Men* should be more bitter; it would be nearer the total truth."

In response, Zora wrote, "We [African people] talk about the race problem a great deal, but go on living and laughing and striving like everybody else." Black people have lives that are more than just reactions to white people, and that's what Zora wanted her writing to show.

With the publication of *Mules and Men,* Zora got some publicity, but not much money. Publishers didn't pay much during the Great Depression. Zora made only $500 from *Mules and Men* during its first five years in print.

In the autumn of 1935, Zora got a job with the New York division of the Federal Theatre Project. The Theatre Project provided jobs for playwrights, actors, and others during the depression. Zora earned $23.86 a week. Although she wasn't making much of a living, Zora could at least celebrate African-American life on stage. She didn't stay with the Theatre Project long though. She was awarded a Guggenheim Fellowship to study West Indian magic. Zora accepted the fellowship on March 18 and quit her job two days later.

Zora left A. W. P. in New York. She had decided that their love was sincere but hopeless. She wanted this collecting trip to help her forget him.

Zora swept into Kingston, Jamaica, in mid-April 1936. Soon afterward, a Kingston newspaper printed a photograph of her in riding pants, hat cocked to the side. She said in the accompanying story that she had only to "squat down awhile and after that things begin to happen. Jamaica is a seething Africa under its British exterior." Her words proved true. While on the island, Zora saw a medicine man silence all the frogs in the jungle with the power of his mind.

Views of the Caribbean Islands in the 1930s, taken by Alan Lomax

In early autumn, Zora went to Haiti. There were so many voodoo (often called hoodoo in the American South) stories, traditions, and rituals there that she didn't know where to start collecting. So she didn't start at all.

Using her leftover feelings for A.W. P. as fuel, Zora composed a love story instead. She wrote steadily for seven weeks. Like Zora, the main character, Janie, is a woman who falls in love with a younger man, Tea Cake.

Zora hit her stride with *Their Eyes Were Watching God,* but sales were only fair. The reading public expected protest and anger from black writers, not a love story from a woman's point of view.

In March of 1937, Zora was awarded a second Guggenheim Fellowship to continue her research in the Caribbean. In Haiti, Zora managed to photograph a woman said to be a zombie—someone who has been brought back from the dead. Then she went too far. Deep in the Haitian bush, Zora nearly died from a violent, unknown illness. Zora believed that she had been poisoned because of her voodoo studies—that someone didn't want her to learn any more.

Zora knew when to quit. She rested for two months, until she was well. In September, she returned to New York to finish writing about her experiences.

Tell My Horse is Zora's account of her experiences with folk magic. Zora treated voodoo as a serious "religion of creation and life," not as superstition.

When Zora went back to Eatonville in April 1938, she became an editor of the Federal Writers' Project for the state of Florida. The Writers' Project was more free of racial discrimination than most of the United States, and it hired several African-American writers and editors.

Zora as the editor of the Florida history division of the Federal Writers' Project

Zora worked mainly on "The Florida Negro," a history of African Americans in Florida. It was never published. On this job, she spent a lot of time out of the office. That helped her stick it out for so long. She would show up at the office, collect her check, and disappear. She also met Albert Price III, a playground worker in Jacksonville, and fell in love again. That helped the time pass too.

In June, Zora and Albert got married. He was twenty-three; she was forty-eight. What worked for Janie and Tea Cake in *Their Eyes Were Watching God* might work for Zora and Albert. Then again, it might not.

In July of 1939, Zora's old high school, now Morgan State University, awarded her an honorary doctor of letters. The degree helped her get a job as the Director of Dramatic Productions at the North Carolina College for Negroes. Zora left Albert in Florida.

The college faculty members were expected not to draw any attention to themselves. Zora drove up in a bright red convertible. And faculty members should certainly live on or near campus. Zora rented a cabin in the mountains outside of town. She and the North Carolina College for Negroes didn't like much of anything about each other. She left at the end of the school year.

In November 1939, Lippincott published Zora's third novel, *Moses, Man of the Mountain*. Zora's Moses is a hoodoo man. It is he who leads his people out of slavery and into the Promised Land.

After her North Carolina experience, Zora was at

loose ends. Albert was still in Florida. He and Zora had never lived together more than two weeks at a stretch. When Zora filed for divorce in February 1940, she claimed that Albert drank, refused to work or maintain a home, and was abusive. For his part, Albert said that Zora had started out promising to send him to college and ended threatening to "fix him" with hoodoo.

Zora then had second thoughts about divorce. She and Albert tried again to make a go of it. He even went with her on a folklore-collecting trip to South Carolina, but it made no difference. Zora's second marriage was over. She returned to New York and stayed until the spring of 1941. She lectured around and visited old friends.

Over the years, Zora had written many articles and essays, in addition to her books. In fact, Zora had had more work published than any other African-American woman, and many people wanted to know more about her. Bertram Lippincott suggested that she write the story of her life. Zora said no at first—her career wasn't over—but then she agreed to write a first volume, which she completed in July 1941.

Zora revised her life story over the next several months and worked briefly as a story consultant for Paramount Studios in California near the end of the year. She did nothing steadily.

The United States entered World War II in December 1941. Zora had written some blunt, unpopular things about the United States in the autobiography she sent to Lippincott. On white Americans' view of democracy, Zora's manuscript read, "One hand in somebody else's pocket and one on your gun and you are highly civilized. Your heart is where it belongs—in your pocket book." On racism, she had written, "[It] would be a good thing for the Anglo-Saxon to get the idea out of his head that everybody owes him something just for being blonde." Her editor took out her boldest statements and toned down the rest.

Zora allowed the censored version to be published. She explained, "Rather than get across all of the things which you want to say you must compromise and work within the limitations [of those people] who have the final authority in deciding whether or not a book shall be printed."

Dust Tracks on a Road, Zora's autobiography, was published in November 1942. As always, Zora hid her innermost thoughts. The book is contradictory, confusing, and funny—just like Zora.

White critics liked *Dust Tracks,* and it sold well. It won the *Saturday Review*'s Anisfield-Wolf Award for contributing to "the field of race relations." Zora was now an official Negro Representative to white people, and white publications sought her opinions. She continued to anger and flabbergast most African Americans. They didn't realize that her work had been censored by her publisher. Zora couldn't please both European and African Americans with the same words.

Zora settled in St. Augustine in the fall of 1942 to write plays, teach part-time at Florida Normal College, and "keep on eating." She was still living hand-to-mouth.

In early 1943, Zora moved to Daytona Beach and bought a twenty-year-old houseboat, the *Wanago.* There she found the solitude she craved. She also found a good place to indulge in one of her passions—fishing. Much of the world was in the middle of World War II. But on the *Wanago,* Zora could "forget for short periods the greed and ultimate brutality of man to man."

For a while, Zora enjoyed herself. In March, Howard University honored her as a distinguished alumna. That spring, Zora went to New York to work on the script of a musical comedy with Dorothy Waring, a white writer. When their work was over, Zora returned to Florida. She then sailed the *Wanago* 1,500 miles up the Atlantic Coast to New York. She tried to drum up money in Manhattan for her and Dorothy's planned musical. The play was never produced, and she sailed back home.

Everette, Jr., a teenager now, aboard Aunt Zora's houseboat. She lived on and off houseboats for six years, enjoying this life for many reasons. One reason was that "all the other boat owners are very nice to me. Not a word about race."

licking
the pots

During the last of the war years, Zora wrote several racial and political articles, in keeping with her new status as an African-American spokeswoman. She also became more and more controversial, especially among her people. In the 1940s, African Americans expected black writers to protest white people's racist treatment of them every chance they got. Zora argued, "I freely admit the handicaps of race in America. But I contend that we are just like everybody else. Black skunks are just as natural as white ones."

In late 1944, Zora got a letter from Reginald Brett, an English miner in British Honduras (now Belize). He described an ancient lost city of the Mayans in the jungle. Zora was intrigued. But she knew nobody would pay her to lead an expedition to find it. So she asked the Guggenheim Foundation and the Library of Congress for money to study the folklore of Honduran Indians.

Her requests were turned down. She spent much of the rest of 1945 in Daytona Beach, Florida, writing a novel and looking for a way to get to British Honduras.

Lippincott eventually rejected her novel, "Mrs. Doctor," and the summer of 1946 found Zora in New York, still trying to make a living. She worked briefly in a political campaign and then spent a lonely winter in a rented room in a cellar. Her landlady's ten-year-old son was so strange that Zora suggested that he needed treatment for his mental health. The woman rejected Zora's advice, and she offered it no more.

Zora was feeling isolated and depressed about her career and life in general. She was fifty-six years old and broke again. "I felt entirely out of place. . . . I got so it was torture for me to go to meet people."

But Zora believed in the new novel she was working on, and in the spring of 1947, she switched publishers. Charles Scribner's Sons advanced her some money for the manuscript, and off she went to British Honduras. Zora didn't mount any trek into the jungle though. She stayed in Puerto Cortés and worked on her novel. That autumn, she finished a draft of *Seraph on the Suwanee* and then reworked it for months. She left Honduras in February 1948 and did the manuscript's final polishing in New York.

In September, the New York police came to Zora's apartment and took her to jail. They charged her with committing an immoral act with her ex-landlady's son. Insulted and angry, Zora asked for a lie-detector test, but the police ignored her.

The truth was that the boy's mother had been offended at Zora's comments nearly two years before. Her child was *not* crazy. To get even, the woman had coaxed her son into lying about Zora. Zora had been in Honduras when most of the incidents were supposed to have taken place. After a thorough investigation, the charge against Zora was dropped.

But an employee of the court leaked the story to the Baltimore *Afro-American* newspaper. The newspaper played the story for all it was worth. The employee who told the newspaper was an African American. Zora wrote that that was "the blow that knocked me loose from all that I have ever looked to and cherished."

"The thing is too fantastic, too evil, too far from reality...," she wrote to Carl Van Vechten. "One inconceivable horror after another swept over me. I went out of myself, I am sure, though no one seemed to notice.... All that I have believed in has failed me. I have resolved to die...."

Zora didn't kill herself. She had gone out of herself, but she came back.

Seraph on the Suwanee had hit the bookstores in October 1948. It had sold well and soon went into a second printing. Sales would have been even better, but many white booksellers in the South wouldn't sell Zora's books. And her arrest had made her afraid of people, so she wouldn't do publicity appearances.

Although the main characters talk like people from Eatonville, *Seraph on the Suwanee* is about white people. Black writers were expected to write about

This photo was used to promote the sales of *Seraph on the Suwanee.*

white people to show that they could write about things common to all humans. Proving that she could write about anybody was at least partly what Zora wanted to do. "I am not so sure that I have done my best, but I tried," Zora wrote to a friend.

Just the same, *Seraph on the Suwanee* was good enough for Scribners to pay Zora $500 for an option on her next novel and $40 a week so she could survive the winter. She lived in Brooklyn with Everette and his family, and continued to write, of course. She managed to sell a few magazine articles.

Perhaps a little discouraged, Zora went home to Florida in July 1949. Fred Irvine, an old friend, had offered to take her to British Honduras on his cargo boat. Zora joined him on board the *Challenger,* and made plans for their trip to Central America.

But Zora had found somebody even worse with money than *she* was. Irvine borrowed money from her and gambled it away on horse races. By January 1950, both of them were broke.

Zora borrowed from her friends and gave a talk to local librarians in order to live, but she was always short of cash. In desperation, Zora began working as a maid in a swank Miami neighborhood for $30 a week plus food and a place to sleep.

In the spring of 1950, a reporter caught Zora working as a maid. While Zora was dusting bookshelves, the owner of the house was reading a short story in the *Saturday Evening Post* written by the maid she thought of as her "girl."

In the summer of 1950, she plunged into politics, working in a campaign and writing opinionated essays. And she was laboring on her eighth book, "The Lives of Barney Turk," a novel about a white man. Scribners turned it down. Zora still didn't have any money, so when friends in Belle Glade offered her a place to stay, she took it.

The *American Legion Magazine* bought an article of Zora's that winter, and she began to look forward to "being under my own roof. . . . Oh, to be once more alone in a house." She was tired of "having to avoid folks who have made me loans so that I could eat and sleep. The humiliation is getting to be much too much for my self-respect."

Zora sold an article to the *Saturday Evening Post* and regained some of her spirit. The *Post* paid well. In June 1951, Zora rented the one-room cabin in Eau Gallie where she had written *Mules and Men.* She bought some secondhand furniture, an icebox, and a new pair of slacks. Now, at least, she didn't have to wash her only dress to have something clean to wear.

Before moving into her Eau Gallie house, Zora had sent "The Golden Bench of God" off to her publisher. It was a novel based on the life of African-American business tycoon Madame C. J. Walker. Two weeks after Zora moved, Scribners rejected the novel.

Zora couldn't have cared less. Her response to her publisher glows: "I am very happily located . . . back in my little house. . . . The place was quite shaggy when I arrived a month ago, but I have the joy of clearing it and arranging things like I please. . . . I am planting butterfly ginger . . . pink verbena and bright colored poppies. Living the kind of life for which I was made, strenuous and close to the soil, I am happier than I have been for at least ten years."

While living in Eau Gallie, Zora wrote several pieces about her dog, Spot, a more-or-less terrier. And she listened to the mockingbirds and cardinals that came to the birdbath and feeder she had set up. Her place was so pretty, tourists stopped to take snapshots.

Zora lived quietly from 1951 to 1956, but her politics were as wild as ever. She hated Communism, and that led her to support right-wing causes, many of which were racist. And Zora was riled at the 1954 Supreme Court decision that led to school desegregation. She said it implied that African-American children couldn't get much from school unless white children were there.

And still she wrote. Zora had become interested in Jewish history as early as 1945. Her research had led her to information about Herod the Great, once king of Judea. The story of Herod's life fascinated Zora, and now she burned to tell it.

In August 1955, Scribners rejected her Herod manuscript. She wrote to her editor, "Please, please do not think that I feel badly. . . . I have . . . faith in the material and . . . my conviction that I can handle it. All is well."

But all wasn't well. The house Zora had been living in was for sale. Zora certainly couldn't buy it with no money. And her landlord didn't want to sell it to her anyway because it was in a white neighborhood. In March 1956, he told her she had to get out. Zora moved to a house trailer on Merritt Island, across the Indian River from Cocoa, Florida.

Zora found work at nearby Patrick Air Force Base as a librarian. She hated it. For keeping track of technical papers, sixty-five-year-old Zora earned $1.88

an hour. Her supervisor agreed that she was "too well educated for the job" when he fired her.

Zora had worked at the base long enough to get $26 a week in unemployment benefits—just enough to get by. Now struggling with the pain from a stomach ulcer, she reworked her Herod manuscript. Zora thought that she had "a greater competence with the tools of my trade. . . ." But Zora was wearing down.

In October, Zora tried to get a job at the Air Force Test Center in Cocoa. She failed. Then in December 1956, C. E. Bolen came to see her. He asked if she would write for his newspaper, the *Fort Pierce Chronicle*. Zora jumped at the chance. She moved to Fort Pierce, Florida, and for a few months, she wrote a column on "Hoodoo and Black Magic."

Zora lived in a little house that she rented for $10 a week from C. C. Benton, her doctor. She had a little yard, and she made the most of it. All year round, she grew tomatoes and collard greens and other vegetables in her garden, so she never went hungry. There were plenty of azaleas, gardenias, and morning glories to look at too. In the evening, the scent of Zora's Cape Jasmine blooms drifted over the neighborhood, just like in Eatonville all those years ago.

In early 1958, Zora tried substitute teaching at Lincoln Park Academy, Fort Pierce's public high school for African Americans. Zora was sixty-seven years old and set in her ways though. She wasn't *about* to go back to school to get a teaching certificate. Her stay was short.

Zora (center) and Spot visiting with some friends

By the late 1950s, Zora wasn't getting around very
well. Zora was fat by this time—over two hundred
pounds. And she had caught a tropical disease in
British Honduras that sometimes sapped her energy
and made her periodic abdominal pain worse. She
stayed away from a family reunion that year, so no one
would find out just how bad off she really was.

Dr. Benton liked Zora, and he would sometimes come
by at the end of his day's work. "My wife and I used to
invite her over to the house for dinner," Benton remembered. "Zora loved to eat. She could sit down
with a mound of ice cream and just eat and talk till it
was all gone." When Dr. Benton learned about Zora's
money problems, he let her rent slide. Zora and Spot
could live rent-free.

In 1959, a clot temporarily blocked a blood vessel in
Zora's brain. Zora had a stroke. Some of her brain
cells died from lack of oxygen, and she couldn't con-

centrate like she used to. Dr. Benton said, "She couldn't really write much near the end. . . . Her mind was affected. She couldn't think about anything for long." In October, Zora had to go live in the Saint Lucie County welfare home.

Zora knew she was dying. Her brother Clifford and his family visited her in January 1960. They and the rest of the Hurstons offered her money, but she refused. Zora felt that anything anybody wanted to do for her they should have done already. Now it was too late to make any difference. She didn't want any fancy funeral. Clifford and the others should spend their money on the living.

Zora Neale Hurston died on January 28, 1960. Years earlier, Zora had thought about her life and written:

> *I can look back and see sharp shadows, high lights, and smudgy inbetweens. I have been in Sorrow's kitchen and licked out all the pots. Then I have stood on the peaky mountain wrapped in rainbows, with a harp and a sword in my hands. . . . What I had to swallow in the kitchen has not made me less glad to have lived, nor made me want to low-rate the human race, nor any whole sections of it. . . . Let us all be kissing-friends. Consider that with tolerance and patience, we godly demons may breed a noble world in a few hundred generations or so. Maybe all of us who do not have the good fortune to meet, or meet again, in this world, will meet at a barbecue.*

After Zora's death, a friend collected money to bury her in an unmarked grave in Fort Pierce's cemetery for African Americans. It seemed fitting. Zora always liked being with her people.

afterword

Writer Alice Walker brought Zora Neale Hurston's work to new readers in the late 1970s. Since then, every book Hurston published has been reprinted, some of them more than once. *Mule Bone* has been performed on Broadway. *Their Eyes Were Watching God* is recognized as a classic. Every January, Eatonville hosts a Zora Neale Hurston Festival of the Arts. College students read Hurston's work for literature classes, and no discussion of African-American writers is complete without her name. At last.

Hurston had some of her problems because the pleasure she got from her African heritage was unusual for her time. When she had to choose between the science of the university and the stories of her people, the stories always won. She had other problems because she was hardheaded. Her ability to keep running after she'd lost her shoes, to strut when others expected her to crawl, was a blessing and a curse. It was a blessing because it kept her going when times were bad, and times were often bad. It was a curse because it separated her from those who had less faith. Jumping at the sun ain't easy.

notes

page 11—Cape Jasmine flowers are also called gardenias.

page 12—In her autobiography, Zora refers to her mother as *Lucy Potts*. A photocopy of her mother's signature from April 26, 1899, shows her name as *Lula Hurston,* and her maiden name as *Lula Pots.*

page 12—A family source says that Lucy Ann Potts Hurston was born December 31, 1865. But the document that she signed as *Lula Hurston* has her age in 1899 as thirty-two.

page 13—Zora wrote that Lucy let another family friend choose the name *Neale*. Census records from 1900 show her as Zora L. Hurston, and a family source says her middle name was *Lee*. Some think *Neale* was from an early, unknown marriage. The truth about her middle name is Zora's secret.

page 14—Recent research indicates that John Hurston was the mayor of Eatonville from 1912 to 1916, not nearly as early as Zora implied.

page 29—In her autobiography, Zora refers to this woman only as Mrs. G----.

page 25—Records are sketchy, and dates until Zora was 26 or so must be estimated. She always lied about her age.

page 32—In her autobiography, Zora refers to this woman only as M----.

page 45—This story is taken from Zora's "Eatonville Anthology," a collection of tales told in Eatonville. It was published in the *Messenger* in 1925.

page 68—Private as always, Zora wrote of this man only as A.W.P.

bibliography

Bambara, Toni Cade. "Some Forward Remarks" to *The Sanctified Church,* a compilation of essays by Zora Neale Hurston. Berkeley: Turtle Island Foundation, 1981.

Bontemps, Arna, ed. *The Harlem Renaissance Remembered.* New York: Dodd, Mead & Company, 1972.

Bush, Trudy Bloser. "Transforming Vision: Alice Walker and Zora Neale Hurston." *The Christian Century,* November 16, 1988, 1035-9.

Gates, Henry Louis, Jr. *Figures in Black.* New York: Oxford University Press, 1987.

Gates, Henry Louis, Jr. Afterword to *Mules and Men,* by Zora Neale Hurston. New York: Harper and Row, 1990.

Hemenway, Robert. *Zora Neale Hurston: A Literary Biography.* Madison: University of Illinois Press, 1977.

Huggins, Nathan. *Harlem Renaissance.* New York: Oxford University Press, 1971.

Hughes, Langston, Milton Meltzer, and C. Eric Lincoln. *A Pictorial History of Blackamericans.* New York: Crown Publishers, Inc., 1973.

Hurston, Zora Neale. *Dust Tracks on a Road.* Madison: University of Illinois Press, 1942.

Hurston, Lucy Ann. Author interviews, 1991.

Jacobson, Lynn. "The Mark of Zora." *American Theatre,* July/August 1990, 24-30.

Lewis, David Levering. "Harlem's First Shining." *Modern Maturity,* February-March 1989, p.56.

Lewis, David Levering. *When Harlem Was in Vogue.* New York: Alfred A. Knopf, 1981.

Locke, Alain, ed. *The New Negro.* New York: Atheneum, 1975.

Lomax, Alan. Author interview, 1991.

Perkins, Kathy A. *Black Female Playwrights.* Bloomington: Indiana University Press, 1989.

Nathiri, N. Y., ed. *Zora!* Orlando: Sentinel Communications Company, 1991.

National Association for the Advancement of Colored People. *Thirty Years of Lynching in the United States 1889-1918.* New York: Arno Press and *The New York Times*, 1969.

Rampersad, Arnold. *The Life of Langston Hughes.* vol. 1. New York: Oxford University Press, 1986.

Story, Ralph D. "Gender and Ambition: Zora Neale Hurston in the Harlem Renaissance." *The Black Scholar,* Summer/Fall 1989, 25-31.

Walker, Alice, ed. *I Love Myself When I Am Laughing... And Then Again When I Am Looking Mean and Impressive.* New York: The Feminist Press, 1979.

Wilson, Margaret F. "Zora Neale Hurston: Author and Folklorist." *Negro History Bulletin,* October/November/December 1982, 109-110.

Wintz, Cary D. *Black Culture and the Harlem Renaissance.* Houston: Rice University Press, 1988.

All unattributed quotations were taken from one of the above sources. Most were selected from Hurston's autobiography, *Dust Tracks on a Road.*

index

about the author

When Mr. Porter was in high school and college, there were no courses and few books about black history and art. So now Mr. Porter writes mostly about African Americans. He takes on complex topics and works to make them clear and lively for both children and adults.

Mr. Porter is the author of six books for children, including *Kwanzaa*, illustrated by Janice Lee Porter. He has written articles, essays, and book reviews for the *Wisconsin Academy Review*, the *Circle* newspaper, and the *Hungry Mind Review*. Mr. Porter is the managing editor of *COLORS: Minnesota's Journal of Opinion by Writers of Color*.

The photographs and illustrations are reproduced courtesy of: The Maitland Art Center (paintings of Eatonville by Jules Andre Smith), cover, back flap of jacket, pp. 10, 18; The Beinecke Rare Book and Manuscript Library, Yale University, front cover oval, pp. 52, 54, 58 (right), 67; Library of Congress, pp. 2, 8, 43 (bottom), 70, 72, 73 (both), 92; The Rare Book and Literary Manuscript Collection, University of Florida Library, Gainesville, pp. 7 (with Stetson Kennedy), 39, 62, 84, 88; Department of College Archives and Special Collections, Olin Library, Rollins College, Winter Park, Florida, p. 14 (top); Winifred Hurston Clark and the Preservation of Eatonville Committee, pp. 14, 31; Florida State Archives, pp. 22-23; Lucy Ann Hurston, pp. 28, 44, 60, 75 (top, taken by Stetson Kennedy), 79; Moorland-Spingarn Research Center, Howard University, pp. 37, 40, 41 (taken by Carl Van Vechten), 42 (invitation for 1925 *Opportunity* contest, designed by Winold Reiss), 58 (left); The Bettmann Archives, p. 43 (top); Schomburg Center for Research in Black Culture, p. 75 (bottom); Columbia University, p. 47; Erik Overby Collection, University of South Alabama Archives, p. 50; The Amistad Research Center, Tulane University, New Orleans, pp. 55, 56; Fisk Archives, Fisk University, p. 83; Janice Lee Porter, p. 96.